The West Somers...

Recollections

Contents

© Colin Howard with Paul Conibeare 2010
Photos: © as credited.
Characters © Ken Kimberley author of *Oi Jimmy Knacker, Heavo Heavo Lash Up & Stow* and *Knock Down Ginger* (Published by Silver Link)

First published in 2010
ISBN 978 1 85794 360 3

Silver Link Publishing Ltd
The Trundle
Ringstead Road
Great Addington
Kettering
Northants NN14 4BW

Tel/Fax: 01536 330588
email: sales@nostalgiacollection.com
Website: www.nostalgiacollection.com
British Library Cataloguing in Publication Data
A catalogue record for this book is available from the British Library.
Printed and bound in Czech Republic

Cover Picture: WATERSMEET On a sunny October evening, GWR 2-8-0 No 3850 hauls a demonstration freight train towards Bishops Lydeard during the 2007 Autumn Steam Gala. *Tom Adams*

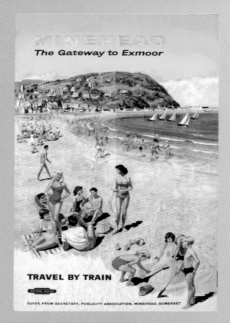

Title page: **MINEHEAD** GWR 2-6-2T No 4561 stands in full steam at Minehead's Bay platform in November 1989. The locomotive was withdrawn from service in 1998 and is currently undergoing overhaul at the West Somerset Railway Association's engineering facility at Williton. The line to the left now runs to the turntable, installed in 2008, and the water tower to the right has been removed. *Alan Turner*

Poster: An iconic image from the days of British Railways. This poster, from the 1950s, was used to advertise the seaside attractions of Minehead for rail travellers, before the days of mass car ownership. British Rail closed the line on 4 January 1971, following the Beeching Report, and it was subsequently reopened to trains as a private railway, the first train being a directors' special that ran from Bishops Lydeard to Minehead on Sunday 21 December 1975. The general public had to wait until the following Spring before they could take their turn. The original poster can be seen in The Gauge Museum at Bishops Lydeard Station and is reproduced by kind permission of the West Somerset Railway Association.

Map: Courtesy of Stephen Edge

Opposite: **MINEHEAD** A view of the former engine shed and water tower taken in April 1938. This area is now a car park and the site of the new station cafe and turntable. The former station cottages, which still exist, can be seen in the background. *M. E. J. Deane, courtesy Ian Bennett*

Acknowledgments

Foreword

by Peter Townsend

It is with a feeling of great admiration that I wish to thank all the photographers who have helped in completing this book on the West Somerset Railway, without whose skill and enthusiasm none of this would have been possible. In particular I am grateful to Paul Conibeare, Alan Turner, Steve Martin, Allan Stanistreet and Tim Stanger of South West Images for their input. I would like to thank our colleagues at the railway and my wife Janet for their support, but most of all I am grateful for the determination and hard work of those early enthusiasts who fought to keep the line alive and make it the success story it is today. The West Somerset Railway is one of the most picturesque railways in the country – I hope that it will continue to thrive as we hold it in trust for future generations. Finally, if I have failed to acknowledge your contribution, I apologise. All photographs not individually credited are by Colin Howard or are taken from the WSR PLC collection.

Early one morning way back in the early 1960s outside the scout hut in Old Town, Swindon, along with fellow members of the 18th Swindon Scout Troop, I climbed aboard the Chas Goodenough removal lorry for the annual summer camping trip. Not for us the cab – we were in the back along with all the tents, haversacks and equipment – that wouldn't be allowed today! This was also to be my first experience of the West Somerset Railway. We spent a week – or was it two? – at a farm near St Audries Bay. Many of the scout troop had relations who worked in the railway works and some were keen to see their work in action. Together with those of us that were railway enthusiasts, a trip on the branch from Watchet to Minehead was high on the agenda! Back then it was very busy – including excursions from many parts of the country.

I have been fortunate to revisit the branch many times in the ensuing 50-plus years. Witnessing its gradual decline up to closure by BR in 1971 was a saddening experience. How marvellous, though, is the contrasting experience today! The authors of this volume – WSR Retail Manager Colin and WSR General Manager Paul – have literally been *Working on the Railroad* for many years and their combined experience and choice of images has captured the enormous progress since 1971, which has resulted in the now thriving and invigorated WSR. The result is a book to be enjoyed by visitors and enthusiasts alike – if I close my eyes I could be back in the Owl Patrol!

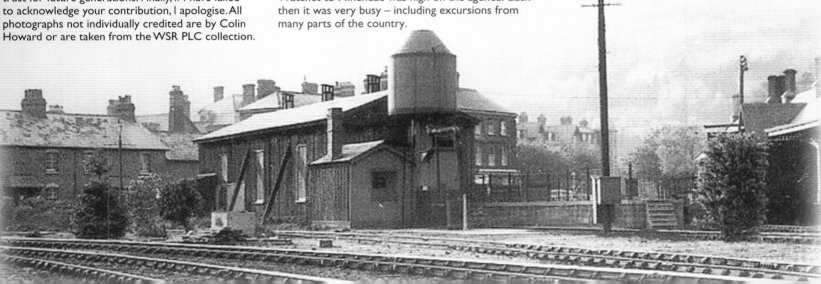

MINEHEAD

Below: **MINEHEAD** awakes to a sunny morning following an apparently rainy night. The platform here was extended in 1934 to accommodate long trains of holidaymakers. Platform One, on the left, is almost a quarter of a mile long and was constructed to be able to accommodate trains of up to 16 carriages; it is now used to accept incoming rail tours from other parts of the UK. *WSR PLC*

Right: **MINEHEAD** A montage of the flower arrangements to be found on the WSR surrounds Somerset & Dorset Joint Railway 2-8-0 No 88 as it awaits service by the locomotive crew. No 88 is owned by the Somerset & Dorset Railway Trust, which is based at Washford Station. The loco has been in regular service on the WSR since its extensive overhaul was completed in 2005. To the rear of the loco is Platform One, where the company offices and gift shop are located. Meanwhile GWR 2-6-2T No 5553 sits over the inspection pit. *Clive Goddard*

Right: **MINEHEAD** A snowy scene outside Minehead Station in early 2010. The booking office can be clearly seen at the entrance to the station adjacent to Minehead seafront. The booking office was constructed with materials from Cardiff Central Station. In the foreground is the information sign erected on completion of the turntable works in 2008. *Martyn Snell*

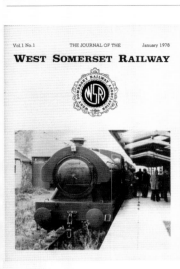

Vol.1 No.1 THE JOURNAL OF THE January 1978

WEST SOMERSET RAILWAY

Left: The front cover of the first edition of the West Somerset Railway Association Journal from January 1978. The Journal is still published and posted out to members on a quarterly basis. The WSRA supports the company in the running of the railway and is based at Bishops Lydeard Station. *WSRA*

Below left: **MINEHEAD** The buffer stops by Minehead seafront. North Hill rises in the background and offers outstanding views of the coastline and of the West Somerset Railway as it heads south from its terminus towards Bishops Lydeard. *Colin Howard*

Below: **MINEHEAD** Early morning at Minehead looking towards the seafront. The tall brown structures amongst the parked cars are lifting jacks, used to lift locomotive frames for an easy and safe method of removing wheelsets. *Colin Howard*

Left: **MINEHEAD** The view of the southern side of the station building. The newly paved pedestrian area was part of the turntable development and allows access to the shop directly from the car park. The area extends to the seafront entrance. *Colin Howard*

Below left: **MINEHEAD** Great excitement in April 1964 as 'Duchess' 4-6-2 No 6229 *Duchess of Hamilton* is unloaded ready to continue its journey to Butlins holiday camp, where it was placed on static display until it was moved to the National Railway Museum in March 1975. *Paul Conibeare collection*

Below: Minehead stands at the northern terminus of the West Somerset Railway, and the station's proximity to the seafront can be seen in this aerial shot. The entrance to the station is to the right of the picture. The sweeping white structure on the far side of the platform canopy is the viewing area for the turntable and the station cafe, which were completed in 2008. The flats to the left are built on the site of the old Minehead Lido, which opened in 1936 and closed in the 1980s. The materials for the seawall and sea defences were brought to Minehead via the WSR in the late 1990s. *Alan Dorrington*

Below: **MINEHEAD** The entrance to Minehead Station and the car park area, photographed in 1923. The main building was extended in the 1930s to incorporate a parcels office. The former entrance to the booking office is behind the parked vehicle. *M. E. J. Deane, courtesy Ian Bennett*

Right: The early days of the West Somerset Railway were often difficult financially and the railway gained considerable publicity as the location for the children's television series *The Flockton Flyer*. GWR 0-6-0 Pannier tank No 6412, which had hauled trains at the opening of the WSR on 28 March 1976, played the starring role in the 1977 series. The film has recently been rediscovered and released as a DVD. The railway has also featured in films, *The Landgirls* and *A Hard Day's Night* being well-known examples.

Far right: **MINEHEAD** Volunteers Malcolm Bernard Ranse and John Sumbler are hard at work on GWR 2-6-2T Prairie No 4561 outside Minehead engine shed in 1977! John Shortland can just be made out sitting inside the smokebox. *Chris Dyer*

BRITAINS LONGEST PRESERVED RAILWAY

Printed in West Somerset by Gull Press.

9th June 1979

Below: **MINEHEAD** Galas and special events are an important part of life on the railway. Over the years many famous locomotives have visited, including *Duke of Gloucester, Tornado, Lord Nelson, Bittern, Royal Scot, King Edward I* and *Evening Star.* Here Class 9F 2-10-0 No 92203 *Black Prince* has just arrived at Minehead Station. Its owner, the famous railway and wildlife artist and conservationist David Shepherd, is seen receiving a souvenir of his visit from WSR PLC Retail Manager Colin Howard at the Spring 2010 Steam Gala. *Keith Sanders*

Below: **MINEHEAD** A semi-derelict Minehead Station in the early 1970s following closure by British Rail Western Region on 4 January 1971. The preservationists moved in shortly after. Note the general air of decay and that some of the track has been removed. Compare this to the current well-kept, heritage station shown in the adjacent picture. *Paul Conibeare collection*

Below left: **MINEHEAD** Minehead Station in 2006. In recent years the chimneys and canopy have been replaced in keeping with the age and style of the station. The railway's Permanent Way gang work hard to keep the line weed-free and in a good state of repair. *WSR PLC*

Below: **MINEHEAD** Locomotive staff are busy preparing engines for a Spring Gala day in 2007. The locos shown are GWR 2-6-2T No 5553, GWR 'Manor' 4-6-0 No 7822 *Foxcote Manor* and GWR 2-8-0T No 4247. No 5553 is owned by The Waterman Railway Heritage Trust and is based on the WSR, while *Foxcote Manor* and No 4247 were visiting from the Llangollen Railway and the Bodmin & Wenford Railway respectively. *WSR PLC*

Left: **MINEHEAD** No 5553 has its smokebox emptied by Chris Tucker in front of the buffers at Minehead seafront in March 2007. Before the works on the sea defences in the late 1990s this area flooded on a regular basis, as can be seen in this view from 1990. *WSR PLC*

Below: **MINEHEAD** The platform at Minehead is large enough to host events for several hundred people. In September each year Somerset CAMRA host a real ale weekend with a selection of fine beers from far and wide. Here visitors are enjoying a beer in the sunshine in 2009. Other events hosted are '*Days Out With Thomas*' in July and a Toy Fair in August. *WSR PLC*

Left: **MINEHEAD** The water tower is shown in its current position, having been removed from the end of the platform in the 1990s. Here locomotives take the opportunity to replenish their supplies of coal and water ready for the journey south to Bishops Lydeard. The distance to the Network Rail junction at Norton Fitzwarren is 23 miles, making this the longest standard gauge heritage railway in Britain. *WSR PLC*

BBC TV invites you to a recording of two popular music programmes

PLATFORM 1		PLATFORM 2
JAZZ TRAIN	**PLATFORM TICKET**	**COUNTRY TRAIN**
The Pete Allen Jazz Band	**MINEHEAD STATION**	Don Leather & Cindy
Frank Evans	**THURSDAY 13th MAY 1982 at 7.30**	The Yellowstone Picnic Band

All Jazz and Country & Western fans welcome   Please dress in country style clothes
ADMISSION BY THIS PLATFORM TICKET ONLY   jeans, checks, Stetsons etc.

Refreshments and Bar available at station Buffet

Below: **MINEHEAD** Former Williton Works Foreman Gareth Winter and an assistant turn SR 'West Country' 4-6-2 No 34046 *Braunton* on the Minehead turntable. The turntable was rescued from Pwllheli in 1977 and brought to Minehead, where it was installed in 2008 as part of a joint redevelopment of the station car park by Somerset County Council, the South West Regional Development Agency, the European Union and the West Somerset Railway. The turntable is manually operated and is balanced on a central bearing. As a result of these improvements, locomotives hauling incoming main-line charters can be turned prior to them leaving the railway, thus making the WSR a more attractive proposition for charter operators. *Braunton* made its first public appearance on the railway in September 2008 following an extensive restoration. The locomotive is based on the WSR and is also used to haul steam charter trains on the main line. *Justin Kerr-Peterson*

Right: **MINEHEAD** Signalman Lawrence Hunt at work in Minehead signal box. Like most heritage railways, the WSR relies heavily on volunteers for the everyday running of the line. Although some staff are paid, the railway would not survive without people like Lawrence giving freely of their time. The Minehead box was originally at Dunster, but was moved along the track in November 1977 to its current position with the start of the present single-line working to Dunster. Access to the line is controlled by token, possession of which ensures that there is only one train on that section of the line at any one time. *WSR PLC*

Right and below left: **MINEHEAD** In the early days of the WSR locomotive traction was supplied by two engines, *Bagnall* 0-6-0ST No 2994 *Vulcan,* in green, and No 2996 *Victor,* in black. These were bought from the Austin Motor Company at Longbridge. Both engines have now departed the line, as they were no longer powerful enough to pull the increasingly long trains. *Paul Conibeare collection*

Below: **MINEHEAD** In June 2009 Class 'A1' 4-6-2 No 60163 *Tornado* was a welcome visitor to the line, drawing in thousands of visitors, many of whom had had their interest ignited by the loco's television appearances on the national news and *Top Gear.* Here it is about to depart with a main-line charter to London on 18 June at the end of its two-week stay. *Brian Pibworth*

Above: **MINEHEAD** The present-day Minehead signal box is transported along the line from Dunster in November 1977. Peckett 0-4-0 No 1163 *Whitehead* is carefully pulling the box under the close supervision of one of the early enthusiasts. *Gordon Harris and Alan Grieve*

Left: **MINEHEAD** Since its foundation the WSR has won many awards, including the middle one from the Heritage Railway Association for the turntable project, and is an official 'Enjoy England' visitor attraction. *Colin Howard*

Right: **MINEHEAD** 'Keep the pavement dry': a water feature at Minehead Station. This is one of the most photographed artefacts on the station and probably dates back to the opening of the station in 1874. *Colin Howard*

Below: **MINEHEAD** The station gift shop at Minehead is situated in the former parcels office. Close examination of the area by the door frames reveals large grooves made by the parcels trolleys as they entered and exited the building. The shop has recently been refitted and is operated by the WSR PLC. The Association has a shop at the other end of the line, at Bishops Lydeard. *Colin Howard*

MINEHEAD An atmospheric shot of GWR 2-8-0 No 3850 sitting over the inspection pit outside Minehead shed. No 3850 has been hired to the West Somerset Railway since the completion of its restoration in early 2006. *Peter Chilcott*

Right: **MINEHEAD** Class 'A1' 4-6-2 No 60163 *Tornado* takes on water in Minehead sidings in June 2009. The West Somerset Railway is also home to the Diesel and Electric Preservation Group, which is based at Williton. Two of the Group's locomotives are seen in the sidings behind *Tornado*. Although mainly a steam railway, diesels play an important role in providing back-up at busy times in the timetable and for winter works trains. The railway also plays host to a Mixed Traction Gala in June of each year. *Brian Pibworth*

Below right: **MINEHEAD** GWR 2-6-0 No 5325 is seen here on the original Minehead turntable in the mid-1950s. Like the turntable installed in 2008, this was manually operated. With the demise of steam, it was removed in the early 1960s when steam finished on the branch. *M. E. J. Deane, courtesy Ian Bennett*

Right: **MINEHEAD** The main platform at Minehead as it is today. The entrance to the shop, situated in the former parcels office, is on the right. The scales used for weighing goods can be seen on the platform adjacent to the first GWR bench. The company workshops are on the left of the picture. *Colin Howard*

Below and above far right: **MINEHEAD** The Great Western Railway and P. & A. Campbell advertised combined rail and sea trips in July 1939, which included trips between Minehead and South Wales. Similar trips still run today using the steamships *Balmoral* and *Waverley*, pictured here. *Alan Turner*

Right: **MINEHEAD** A timetable from the early days of preservation in 1977 offering trips along the line. This was just a year after the reopening of the line as the West Somerset Railway in 1976, following its closure by British Rail in 1971.

Right: **MINEHEAD** A typical Great Western branch-line scene showing a GWR Pannier tank about to depart with a stopping train to Taunton. *WSR PLC*

Below: **MINEHEAD** In 1961 GWR 2-6-2 Prairie tank No 4193 approaches Minehead Station in a scene that has changed radically from today. Butlins holiday camp now stands to the left of the picture and the relief road, Seaward Way, now crosses the line behind the train. *M. E. J. Deane, courtesy Ian Bennett*

Below right: **MINEHEAD** A scene from about 1986, showing two DMUs in the Bay sidings, both of which have now moved away from the railway. The two railway staff pictured are Steve Martin, left, and Trevor Barnett on the right. Both are still involved on the railway, Steve as the company's Operating Superintendent and Trevor as an engine driver. *WSR PLC*

Dunster

Left: **DUNSTER** A typical busy day with WSR 2-6-0 No 9351 approaching Dunster with a down train from Bishops Lydeard. The station building is Grade 2 listed and was modelled by Hornby for its station range. The building is unusually grand as it was built for the use of the Luttrell family of Dunster Castle. *Martyn Snell*

Below: **DUNSTER** An aerial shot showing the compact and well-laid-out country station. The former station master's house is hidden in the trees behind the station building. The house was built in 1899 and the station itself dates back to 1874. The goods shed is prominent in the foreground and is still used by the railway's track maintenance team. *Alan Dorrington*

Left **DUNSTER** A view from Dunster Castle showing the railway's close proximity to the coast. A train heads south towards Blue Anchor in March 2008. *Keith Smith*

early 1970s. The 'clippie' here is Graham Hooper. The service is provided free of charge on Bank Holidays and special occasions. *Alan Grieve*

Above: **DUNSTER** Gala time at Dunster in April 2007 sees No 5553 recreating a long-lost scene of wagon shunting at a country station. *WSR PLC*

Right: **DUNSTER** Dunster Station Master Roy Dunglison sees off one of the vintage buses supplied by Quantock Motors, which provide a connecting service to Dunster village for WSR train ticket holders. This particular bus was used by Stockport Corporation until the

Left: **DUNSTER** Another of the vintage buses that serve Dunster Station. This time it is seen in the centre of Dunster village near the famous Yarn Market. *Alan Grieve*

Below: **DUNSTER** GWR 0-4-2 No 1450 engages in further shunting at a gala event, showing the restored Grade 2 listed goods shed behind. *Alan Turner*

Right: Driver Alan Dorrington takes a break on the footplate of No 3850. Eagle-eyed readers may have spotted Alan on television in the popular series *Casualty* and *Doctor Who*. *Ian Smith*

Below: **DUNSTER** A Class 115/117 DMU departs from Dunster on its way to Blue Anchor in 2009. The scene here will have changed little since the days of British Rail. In the background is Dunster Castle, which was owned by the Luttrell family, one of the original founding shareholders of the railway. *Andrew Padfield*

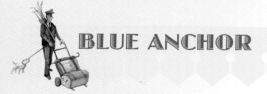

BLUE ANCHOR

Right: **BLUE ANCHOR** The level crossing adjacent to the station can be seen to the right of the picture. Many holidaymakers will use the railway to travel around West Somerset and leave their cars behind. To the bottom of the picture, on the seafront, is an old pill box left over from the Second World War defences. *Alan Dorrington*

Right: **BLUE ANCHOR** Super-power at Ker Moor. The last steam locomotive built by British Railways, Class 9F 2-10-0 No 92220 *Evening Star*, approaches Blue Anchor's home signal in 1989. The presence of *Evening Star* increased the profile of the railway and led to the first running of ten-coach trains. The loco was hired from the National Railway Museum at York. *Alan Turner*

Below: **BLUE ANCHOR** Departing from Blue Anchor, *Black Prince* heads for Dunster with a 2010 Spring Steam Gala train. The proximity to the coast at this point makes it a popular location for photographers and other sightseers. *Alan Turner*

Below: **BLUE ANCHOR** WSR 2-6-0 No 9351 was rebuilt in the workshops at Minehead from GWR 2-6-2 tank engine No 5193. Here it departs from Blue Anchor Station in June 2007 and heads along Ker Moor towards Minehead. Visible by the locomotive are the large blocks of stone that were used as an early form of sea defence. *Alan Turner*

Right: **BLUE ANCHOR** The hills of Exmoor rise up behind a Minehead-bound train in May 2010. The Exmoor National Park includes Dunster village and is a popular destination for walkers and lovers of the countryside. *Alan Turner*

Above and left: **BLUE ANCHOR** A DMU waits for a down train to clear the single track before it can proceed on its way to Washford. The crossing gates are one of the last examples of wheel-operated gates in the South West and date from 1904. *Alan Turner*

Above: **BLUE ANCHOR** Signalman and railway author Richard Derry is about to exchange the token with the fireman of the incoming up train to Bishops Lydeard in September 2009. *Ian Smith*

Far left above: **BLUE ANCHOR** A busy scene at Blue Anchor Station in 1985. Little seems to have changed in the 20 years between these two pictures.

Far left below: Note that the roof of the signal box looks to be in better condition in this later picture and a corrugated building has been constructed on the left-hand side. *WSR PLC (1985) and Keith Smith (2006)*

Left: **BLUE ANCHOR** Filming by a Japanese film crew takes place in 1988. The crew spent most of the day filming the valve gear of the locomotive; the General Manager is still waiting to view the footage taken that day! *Paul Conibeare*

Below: **BLUE ANCHOR** Blue Anchor is a fine example of a well-cared-for heritage railway station. Its appearance is due to the hard work of a small army of volunteers and a credit to the station master and his staff. *Keith Smith*

Opposite page: **BLUE ANCHOR** A driver's-eye view of the newly relaid level crossing and the road ahead from the cab of 'Manor' Class 4-6-0 No 7802 *Bradley Manor*, which was visiting the railway during the Autumn Steam Gala of 2009. Minehead can be seen in the right distance. The signal box is a typical GWR example, and was opened in 1904. *Gerald Peacock*

Left: **BLUE ANCHOR** Driver Paul Conibeare and Fireman Peter Wootten are shown on the footplate of 'Manor' Class 4-6-0 No 7828 *Odney Manor*. *Odney Manor* was purchased by the WSR in 2004 and has undergone an extensive restoration before re-entering traffic on the railway.

Top right: **BLUE ANCHOR** Old meets not so old at Blue Anchor Station. Diesel-hydraulic Class 52 No 1010 *Western Campaigner* pulls into the station as No 5553 awaits its arrival. *Western Campaigner* was used extensively on BR's Western Region from 1962 until 1977. It was saved from the scrapyard by Foster Yeoman Ltd and is now based at the Diesel and Electric Preservation Group at Williton. *Beverley Zehetmeier*

Above: **BLUE ANCHOR** New-build locomotive *Tornado* draws in the crowds at Blue Anchor. During its two-week visit in June 2009 the railway benefited from an additional 7,000 passengers and an unrecorded number of spectators! *fotophile69*

WASHFORD

Above: **BLUE ANCHOR** The signal box basks in the late evening Autumn sunshine. The level crossing gates can sometimes be a challenge to local motorists as they are surprised to find them closed as they approach from the seafront. *Andrew Townsend*

Below: **OLD CLEEVE** A locomotive tackles the hard climb from Blue Anchor to Washford, which can be a test for locomotive crews on a wet day. The pretty village of Old Cleeve and its church is in the background and behind is the Bristol Channel. *Alan Turner*

Above: **WASHFORD** No 5553 works hard on the climb up Washford Bank heading towards Washford Station. The hills of Exmoor are coated in snow in this wintry scene. *Alan Turner*

Right: **WASHFORD** Washford Station is the headquarters of the Somerset & Dorset Railway Trust, and is managed by the Trust on a long-term lease from the WSR. The Trust has a small shop and museum here, staffed by the Trust's volunteers. The WSR benefits from the arrangement by hiring the services of S&DJR No 88 from the Trust. *Alan Dorrington*

Left: **WASHFORD** 'Every schoolboy's dream': a member of the photographer's family looks on longingly as No 9351 runs into Washford Station. Rolling stock owned and maintained by the Somerset & Dorset Railway Trust is stabled at this station. *Stephen Edge*

Below left **WASHFORD** No 3850 is at Kentsford on the long climb from Watchet to Washford. This is a popular location for photographers as the locomotives are working hard at this point. *Alan Turner*

WATCHET

Minehead was opened in July 1874. The length from Bishops Lydeard to Watchet was opened in 1862 as a branch of the Bristol & Exeter Railway, which became part of the Great Western Railway in 1876. *Alan Turner*

Above right: **WATCHET** The WSR here runs alongside the recently rebuilt marina at Watchet Harbour. In former times the harbour was used for the import of esparto grass for the local paper mill, which is still one of the area's major employers. *Alan Dorrington*

Right: **WATCHET** No 4160 departs from Watchet Station and heads north towards Washford. The station building here is side-on to the line as it was once the terminus of the railway from Norton Fitzwarren. The extension to

DONIFORD HALT

Main picture: **DONIFORD** Having just cleared Doniford Halt, GWR 'Hall' Class 4-6-0 No 4936 *Kinlet Hall* travels south towards Williton across Water Lane Bridge during the Spring Gala of 2009. The interesting rock formations on Doniford beach can be seen behind the holiday homes of Doniford Bay. The presence of the cameramen seems to confirm that this was taken during a gala event. *Alan Turner*

Far left: **DONIFORD HALT** No 9351 slows down to stop at the halt. The GWR pagoda building was recovered from the Exe Valley Railway and erected by the WSR in 1988. *Alan Turner*

Left: **DONIFORD HALT** GWR Pannier tank 0-6-0 No 6412 and autocoach 168 complete a classic Great Western branch-line scene in 2005. The plush interior of the autocoach offers a completely different experience from travelling on the more modern coaches of the 1950s and 1960s. *WSR PLC*

Right: **DONIFORD HALT** No 3850, on a Steam Engineman's Course, has just shut off and is slowing down to stop at the halt. Doniford Halt was not an original stopping point on the branch in BR days, but was recovered from Montacute near Yeovil and installed here in 1988 to serve the local holiday camp, which is now run by Haven Holidays. In a new venture, holidaymakers can purchase their tickets from the camp, as there is no ticket office at Doniford. *Alan Turner*

Left: **DONIFORD HALT**
'Western' Class 52 No D1062 *Western Courier* passes Hellwell Bay on its way to Doniford Halt. This area of the coastline is the subject of constant erosion. *Ian Smith*

WILLITON

Below left: **WILLITON** An aerial view of the site at Williton Station. The large white building in the centre of the picture is the 'Tarmac Swindon Shed', which was brought from the former GWR Works at Swindon in 1992. It is now the home of West Somerset Restoration, a subsidiary of the West Somerset Railway Association. *Alan Dorrington*

Below: This is the shed at Swindon, prior to its removal to Williton. Tarmac had wanted to demolish the building, but as it was listed they agreed to dismantle it and re-erect it on the West Somerset Railway. *Paul Conibeare collection*

Above: **WILLITON** A view of the inside of the shed, showing 'West Country' Class No 34046 *Braunton* being observed by a group on a Steam Engineman's Course. The locomotive was returned to traffic in 2008 having undergone an extensive restoration. *Alan Meade*

Above left: **WILLITON** GWR Prairie tank No 4561 heads into Williton Station with an up train from Minehead on its return-to-steam special in November 1989. The area on the left is where the Swindon shed is now situated. *Alan Turner*

Left: **WILLITON** Another view of the site of the Swindon shed prior to its erection. *Paul Conibeare collection*

Left: **WILLITON** The Williton signalman prepares to exchange tokens with the crew of Somerset & Dorset 7F 2-8-0 No 88 as it approaches Williton. The signal box here is one of the original Bristol & Exeter Railway buildings from the 1870s. *fotophile69*

Below left: **WILLITON** Williton Station looking towards Stogumber The bridge, which replaced an earlier wooden structure in 1913, was removed in the late 1960s. *WSR PLC*

Below: **WILLITON** No 3850 takes an up train to Bishops Lydeard. The double track here allows for the trains to pass and is approximately halfway along the line. There are only three passing loops along the line, the others being at Blue Anchor and Crowcombe Heathfield. *Ian Smith*

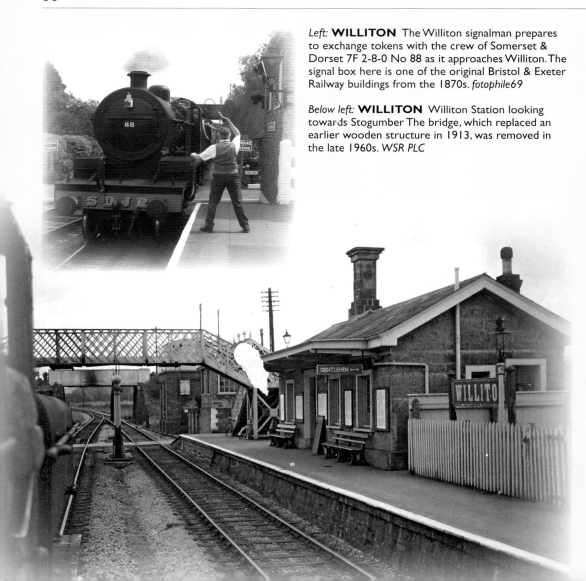

Left: **WILLITON** No 88 approaches Williton Station with a Santa Express in December 2005. These trains offer an extremely novel way to see Santa and receive a present from him and his elves while riding on the train. The railway also runs Santa trains to grottoes at Blue Anchor and Crowcombe Heathfield. Each year some 5,000 children receive a present from Santa on these West Somerset Railway trains. *WSR PLC*

Below left: **WILLITON** The station at Williton is a credit to the volunteers who are responsible for its upkeep. In this summer scene from 2006, looking towards Minehead, the hanging baskets make a wonderful display of colour. *Keith Smith*

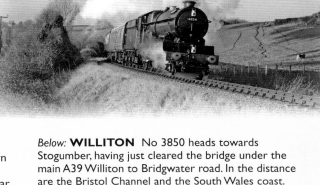

Above right: **WILLITON** GWR 'King' Class 2-6-0 No 6024 *King Edward I* is shown powering out of Williton on the climb towards Stogumber. This location, at Castle Hill, is a popular place for photographers. *Alan Turner*

Below: **WILLITON** No 3850 heads towards Stogumber, having just cleared the bridge under the main A39 Williton to Bridgwater road. In the distance are the Bristol Channel and the South Wales coast. *Alan Turner*

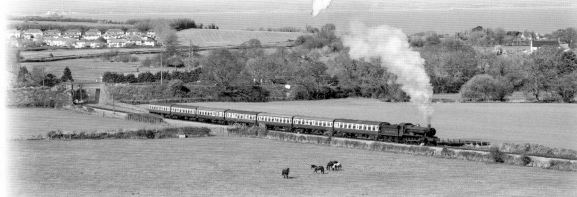

Main picture: **BICKNOLLER** *Tornado* hauls a London-bound charter near Bicknoller Bridge in June 2009, negotiating the series of bends to the obvious lack of interest of a pair of local horses. *Tornado* visited the railway for two weeks in June 2009 and proved a very popular attraction, increasing greatly the numbers of visitors to the railway. *Gill Southwood*

Below: **COTTIFORD BRIDGE** No 5553 gets up a head of steam as it passes Cottiford Bridge near Bicknoller en route to Bishops Lydeard. *Alan Turner*

Below right: **COTTIFORD** S&DJR No 88 has just cleared Cottiford Bridge on its way south to Stogumber with an up train from Minehead. *Kelvin Lumb*

STOGUMBER

Main picture: BICKNOLLER A Bishops Lydeard-bound train steams through the stunning landscape of the Quantock Hills near to Bicknoller. These traditional road signs are still a common feature of the Somerset countryside. *Stephen Edge*

Left: **STOGUMBER** A DMU from Bishops Lydeard approaches Stogumber Station, which is a superb example of a country railway station. It offers good local walks and the village is just a short walk from the station. The gardens in the foreground are situated on the site of the former goods shed and offer a picnic area and seats for the weary traveller. Harry and Iris Horn were station masters here for many years until Iris's death in 2009. A platform waiting room has recently been installed by RAMS, the volunteer maintenance team who are based at Bishops Lydeard. *Alan Turner*

BICKNOLLER

SAMPFORD BRETT

YELLOW
STOGUMBER

CAPTON 1½
MONKSILVER 1¾

Right: **STOGUMBER** GWR No 5553 pulls into Stogumber Station with an up train to Bishops Lydeard. The area to the right of the picture is now a picnic area and garden. In recent times there has been much cutting back of the trees and bushes, which has made the area much lighter. A wooden waiting room has since been constructed on the platform. *Ken Davidge*

Below: **STOGUMBER** A busy scene outside Stogumber Station building. Inside there is a small shop selling souvenirs, second-hand books, teas, coffees and cream teas. It is a real treat to sit in the garden and relax with a snack while listening to the varied bird life. The Station Master, Jenny Davidge, has a great sense of humour and offers visitors wonderful hospitality. *Ken Davidge*

Below right: **STOGUMBER** Class 9F 2-10-0 No 92203 *Black Prince* stops at Stogumber during a busy Spring Gala in March 2010. The smoke coming from the chimney of the station building indicates the presence of a welcoming fire within. An attractive display of daffodils is visible by the picket fence. *Ken Davidge*

Far right: **STOGUMBER** Driver John Farley waits for the right away on the footplate of Class 9F 2-10-0 No 92212 at Stogumber Station. The loco was visiting from the Mid Hants Railway and was part of the British Railways Standards theme of the Spring Gala of 2010. *Ken Davidge*

Below and right: **STOGUMBER** BR Standard 4MT 2-6-4 tank No 80104 approaches Stogumber Station and is preparing to stop to take on passengers. The line of white objects to the right of the loco are distance markers for the driver, helping down trains travelling towards Minehead to stop at the correct place. As seen in the picture above right there used to be a goods shed where the garden is today. *Ken Davidge/M. E. J. Deane, courtesy Ian Bennett*

Below right: **STOGUMBER** S&DJR No 88 is pictured at Water Bridge with a winter train towards the end of the running season on 31 December 2008. The white of the trees and grass is a hard frost rather than snow, which nevertheless provides a rare view of a WSR loco pictured in a wintry scene. *Alan Turner*

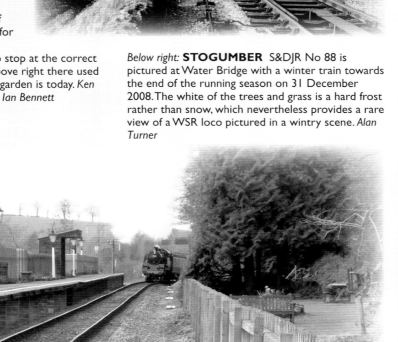

CROWCOMBE HEATHFIELD

Left: **CROWCOMBE HEATHFIELD** WSR 2-6-0 No 9351 is at Crowcombe Heathfield awaiting the arrival of an up train to Bishops Lydeard. Crowcombe Heathfield is the last passing point before the southern terminus of the line at Bishops Lydeard Station, and is a popular stop for walkers and lovers of the countryside. No 9351 was rebuilt at the company engineering works at Minehead, having started life as GWR 2-6-2T No 5193. The current specification of the locomotive is more suited to the needs of the railway and is one of only two steam locomotives owned by the WSR PLC itself. *Beverley Zehetmeier*

Left: **CROWCOMBE HEATHFIELD** No 4160 pulls into a busy Crowcombe Heathfield Station with a down train from Bishops Lydeard. This is the highest above sea level of all the West Somerset Railway stations, and is beautifully kept by the Friends of Crowcombe Heathfield Station. It also welcomes Santa and his elves in December, when several hundred children visit him in his grotto. Events like this help the railway to lengthen the normal tourist season and provide lots of young people and their parents with a magical memory of the railway. *Julian Moore*

Above: **CROWCOMBE HEATHFIELD** GWR 0-6-0T No 6695 leaves Crowcombe Heathfield in bright Autumn sunshine. The locomotive was on hire from the 6695 Locomotive Group based at the Swanage Railway. *Julian Moore*

Below: **CROWCOMBE HEATHFIELD** Station staff discuss the issues of the day outside the rather grand station building. The station has starred in several productions including *The Landgirls*, *A Hard Day's Night* and *The Lion, the Witch and the Wardrobe*. The station has a booking office, which has recently reopened after 40 years, and a small shop selling souvenirs and local produce. *WSR PLC*

Top left: **CROWCOMBE HEATHFIELD** Signalman Freddie Orchard operates the levers in Crowcombe Heathfield signal box, which is a fine example of a GWR wooden box and originally came from Ebbw Vale. The original box here was demolished by British Rail in 1967 and, since its arrival at Crowcombe in 1986, the new one has been lovingly restored to its former glory. Signalmen will always use a cloth to grip the levers to prevent them going rusty. *Tim Stanger, South West Images*

Top right: **CROWCOMBE HEATHFIELD** Class 14 'Teddy Bear' D9526 and Class 25 D7523 *John F. Kennedy* are waiting to depart during a busy Mixed Traction Gala in June 2009. *Keith Smith*

Bottom left: **CROWCOMBE HEATHFIELD** There is a magnificent display of daffodils on a beautiful Spring day as No 34046 *Braunton* approaches the station in March 2010. *Tim Stanger, South West Images*

Bottom right: **CROWCOMBE HEATHFIELD** *Braunton* awaits the arrival of No 88 before continuing its journey to Bishops Lydeard. *fotophile69*

Bottom left: **CROWCOMBE HEATHFIELD** A wintry scene at Crowcombe Heathfield in December 2006. This image graced a Christmas card, which was available from the railway souvenir shops and proved to be extremely popular. *John Ayres*

Middle top **CROWCOMBE HEATHFIELD** GWR No 4160 pulls into Crowcombe Heathfield Station. The lineside is rich in flora and fauna, and occasionally the railway runs 'wildlife trains', with a guide giving a talk on what can be seen along the line. *Alan Tupman*

Middle lower: **CROWCOMBE HEATHFIELD** Newly restored S&DJR No 88 steams through the West Somerset countryside in October 2006. *Claire Rickson*

Top left: **CROWCOMBE HEATHFIELD** A busy scene at Crowcombe Heathfield as S&DJR No 88 awaits the return of visitors to Santa's Grotto in December 2008. *WSR PLC*

Middle left: **CROWCOMBE HEATHFIELD** GWR No 9351 gets up a good head of steam as it passes Nethercott Bridge with a down train to Minehead. *Tim Stanger, South West Images*

Above: **CROWCOMBE HEATHFIELD** LMS 'Royal Scot' 4-6-0 No 6100 *Royal Scot* was a feature of the 2009 Spring Steam Gala, and was its first appearance anywhere since it had undergone a complete restoration having been sold to Bressingham Steam Museum in 1989 by Butlins, Skegness, where it had been on static display since 1978. The loco's crimson livery made a welcome change to the green or black usually in evidence on the West Somerset. Here it passes Nornvis Bridge. *Brian Pibworth*

BISHOPS LYDEARD

BISHOPS LYDEARD is the southern terminus of the West Somerset Railway, although a halt has now been constructed towards the junction with the main line. In the days of British Rail, Bishops Lydeard was the first stop along the branch line. It is now the headquarters of the West Somerset Railway Association, the group that supports the WSR PLC in the day-to-day running of the railway. The railway's museum, The Gauge Museum, is based here and is in the capable hands of Ian Coleby, who wrote a definitive history of the pre-preservation days of the line. Bishops Lydeard also boasts a fine souvenir and model railway shop, and a cafe.

Top left: **BISHOPS LYDEARD** SR No 34046 *Braunton* heads through Churchlands on its way to Bishops Lydeard on a sunny Autumn day in 2008. *Peter Slater*

Middle left: **BISHOPS LYDEARD** GWR No 5553 is seen passing Stones Wood. *Peter Slater*

Bottom left: **BISHOPS LYDEARD** LMS No 6100 *Royal Scot* crosses Combe Florey Bridge with a Spring Gala train on 26 March 2009. *fotophile69*

Below: **BISHOPS LYDEARD** GWR 'Castle' Class 4-6-0 No 5029 *Nunney Castle* and its support coach prepare to run round and couple up to the set of carriages on the left of the picture in April 2005. Alongside these carriages are the station shop, cafe, waiting room and signal box. On the right, adjacent to No 5029, are the administrative offices of the WSRA and The Gauge Museum. Taunton Model Railway Club has an award-winning layout next to the museum. *WSR PLC*

Left: **BISHOPS LYDEARD** Driver Derek Boswell and the owner of the locomotive, Peter Weaver, look back from the footplate of GWR 'Hall' Class 4-6-0 No 4936 *Kinlet Hall* during the Autumn Gala of 2004. The loco is in good steam and they appear to be awaiting a signal from the Guard that the train is ready to leave for Minehead. *Gerald Peacock*

Below left: **BISHOPS LYDEARD** A Class 108 DMU runs into Bishops Lydeard Station with an evening train from Minehead in 2007. The station is deserted but for two members of staff at the ends of the platforms. During train movements visitors are obliged to use the road bridge to cross from one platform to the other, otherwise they may use the foot crossing, which is barrier controlled and manned by station staff. *Claire Rickson*

Below right: **BISHOPS LYDEARD** The railway is a major contributor to the economy of Somerset. It brings in thousands of visitors per year and is thus an important player in the tourism industry of the

West Country. Here two reporters from regional television news make a report from the platform at Bishops Lydeard before a Gala event. *WSR PLC*

Left: **BISHOPS LYDEARD** An interesting view onto the footplate of S&DJR No 88 as it waits with a Santa train at Bishops Lydeard. It takes several hours to heat up the boilers of steam locomotives and this requires footplate staff to begin work in the early hours of the morning to ensure the loco is ready for use. *Tim Stanger, South West Images*

Left: **BISHOPS LYDEARD** This was No 34046 *Braunton* in April 1996, pictured at Bishops Lydeard Station awaiting restoration. Note the graffiti and the board appealing for funds to assist the WSRA in its task of raising enough money to fund the restoration. Thanks to a change of ownership and the subsequent input of private funds, *Braunton* appeared in all its glory at the Autumn Steam Gala of 2008. *Alan Meade*

Top right: **NORTON FITZWARREN** Access to the main line has allowed the unloading and recycling of ballast from the national network to take place at Norton Fitzwarren. *Leonard Renwick*

Below: **NORTON FITZWARREN** In the early days of preservation the limit of the WSR was marked by a sleeper lying across the line just prior to its junction with the West of England main line. In the last few years much work has been done to secure access to the main line and thus enable charters and other traffic to access WSR metals. *Paul Conibeare*

Middle right: **NORTON FITZWARREN** Much of this recycled ballast has been used in the construction of a turning triangle adjacent to the main line. In this aerial view, the main line is at the bottom of the picture and the ballast train can be seen at the top. The triangle is being constructed by volunteers of the WSRA, and will allow whole trains to be turned at this end of the line. This greatly enhances the attractiveness of the WSR for charter traffic and also gives additional benefits, such as the opportunity to even out wheel wear.

Bottom right: **NORTON FITZWARREN** A halt has also been constructed here, seen in June 2010, which allows visitors to use the railway to visit the WSRA's Steam Fair in adjacent fields. In a vote amongst visitors to a WSR website, the new junction was given the name Barnstaple Junction, in recognition of the use of part of the former Barnstaple branch trackbed in the triangle. *Alan Dorrington*

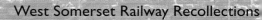

INDEX

Above: **BISHOPS LYDEARD** Firemen, John Panting and Roger Sanders, enjoy a short break and chat with passengers from the footplate of No 34046 *Braunton* in the Summer of 2009. *Ian Smith*

Background: **BISHOPS LYDEARD** No 5553 runs round at a snowy Bishops Lydeard on 29 December 2005. *Claire Rickson*